GAME

GAME

JOAN SULLIVAN

BREAKWATER
P.O. Box 2188, St. John's, NL, Canada, A1C 6E6
WWW.BREAKWATERBOOKS.COM

COPYRIGHT © 2018 Joan Sullivan

LIBRARY AND ARCHIVES CANADA CATALOGUING IN PUBLICATION

Sullivan, Joan, 1963-, author
    Game / Joan Sullivan.

ISBN 978-1-55081-719-5 (softcover)

1. Reach for the top (Competition). 2. Newfoundland and Labrador--Intellectual life--20th century. 3. Newfoundland and Labrador--Social life and customs--20th century. 4. School contests--Social aspects--Newfoundland and Labrador. 5. School contests--Canada. 6. Television quiz shows--Social aspects--Newfoundland and Labrador. 7. Television quiz shows--Canada.
I. Title.
FC2169.S85 2018   971.8'04   C2018-900355-3

ALL RIGHTS RESERVED. No part of this publication may be reproduced, stored in a retrieval system or transmitted, in any form or by any means, without the prior written consent of the publisher or a licence from The Canadian Copyright Licensing Agency (Access Copyright). For an Access Copyright licence, visit www.accesscopyright.ca or call toll free to 1-800-893-5777.

We acknowledge the support of the Canada Council for the Arts, which last year invested $153 million to bring the arts to Canadians throughout the country. We acknowledge the financial support of the Government of Canada and the Government of Newfoundland and Labrador through the Department of Tourism, Culture, Industry and Innovation for our publishing activities.

Printed and bound in Canada.

Canada Council for the Arts   Conseil des Arts du Canada   Newfoundland Labrador   Canada

Breakwater Books is committed to choosing papers and materials for our books that help to protect our environment. To this end, this book is printed on a recycled paper that is certified by the Forest Stewardship Council®.

MIX
Paper from responsible sources
FSC
www.fsc.org   FSC® C004071

*With special thanks to my cousin,
Michael Sullivan*

CONTENTS

3	Introduction
6	Cast and Crew
9	1974
15	SCENE ONE: One generation after
33	SCENE TWO: "This is the game of the year"
41	SCENE THREE: "Well, sirs, let's check the scores"
65	SCENE FOUR: That was when we lost the game [Take 1]
71	SCENE FIVE: That was when we lost the game [Take 2] or And then the buzzer went, and I leapt up
101	SCENE SIX: Lifted up, looking ahead
114	Cast Notes
117	References

INTRODUCTION

"We were the first generation of Newfoundlanders to be Canadian, we were so happy that we would have the opportunities that came with being Canadian. But then, suddenly we were the joke people; the word on the street was that we were a drag on the Canadians, despite statistical evidence to the contrary.

"But we were also quite aware that we had something very, very unique. We had a great and amazing and trenchant use of the English language, a phenomenal musical tradition, and economically we had survived in an interesting and sometimes swashbuckling way."

–Andy Jones, speaking at the Shakespeare in Newfoundland conference, September 30, 2017

1974 marked the twenty-fifth anniversary of Newfoundland's Confederation with Canada. The generation born on the cusp of that union were now busy generating what would come to be known as the "Newfoundland Renaissance," a term coined by journalist and writer Sandra Gwyn. In the first few years of that decade, Breakwater Books, the island's first commercial publisher, was founded; *All Around the Circle* and *Ryan's Fancy* were broadcast on local TV (while Harry Hibbs had a show in Ontario); George Story, William Kirwin, and John Widdowson were at work compiling the *Dictionary of Newfoundland English*, while Percy Janes's *House of Hate*, Cassie Brown's *Death on the Ice*, and Kevin Major's anthology *Doryloads* had just been published; Gerald Squires, Mary Pratt, Christopher Pratt, David Blackwood, Reginald Shepherd, and Helen Parsons Shepherd were painting and printmaking and sculpting; and CODCO was founded as a theatrical revue.

Joseph R. Smallwood, the revered, reviled Only Living Father of Confederation, was, after more than two decades as premier, finally wrestled away from the political helm. Smallwood had dominated every government policy decision, cabinet meeting discussion, and news headline in the province since 1949. What would happen now?

Against this backdrop, and as part of the twenty-fifth anniversary celebrations, the *Reach for the Top* national championship games were moved to St. John's. Newfoundland and Labrador was represented by Gonzaga High School. No Newfoundland team had ever won the championship, and the young Gonzaga team was very much the underdog.

This is the narration of a game that Newfoundlanders gathered around their television sets to watch as a point of cultural hope and pride. And the players' voices are here, as are those of their rival team. It is also an oral portrait of 1974, sketched in the words of Liberal party leader Edward Roberts, Gonzaga teacher Ken Coffey, cultural bureaucrat John Perlin, politician and author Bill Rowe, and provincial and later federal cabinet minister John Crosbie.

CAST & CREW

For Gonzaga: Peter Chafe, Tom Harrington, Sethu Reddy, Gerry Beresford

For Bishop O'Leary: Tim Black, Brian Mader, Pat Bendin, Ihor Gowda

From *Reach for the Top*: Bob Cole, Bill Guest

And featuring:

Ken Coffey, former Gonzaga student and teacher

John Crosbie, provincial and federal politician and cabinet member, author

John Perlin, former director of Cultural Affairs for the province of Newfoundland and organizer of the twenty-fifth anniversary celebrations.

Edward Roberts, politician (Liberal) and Leader of the Opposition at that time

Bill Rowe, provincial politician, broadcaster, and author

1974

The world's population is four billion.

After a record eighty-four days in orbit, the crew of *Skylab 4* returns to Earth.

Patti Hearst, daughter of publisher Randolph Hearst, is kidnapped. About two months later, Hearst, now called Tania, is photographed wielding an MI carbine while robbing a bank in San Francisco.

"The Troubles" in Ireland reach a ferocious peak in ongoing UVF and IRA bombing campaigns with two pub bombings in Birmingham, England, that kill twenty-one and were believed to be the work of the Provos. The Birmingham Six are later sentenced to life, but after a lengthy campaign their convictions are quashed.

Richard Nixon resigns.

Philip Petit walks a high wire between the twin towers of the World Trade Center.

The worst plane crash in history occurs when Turkish Airlines Flight 981, en route from Paris to London, crashes in a wood near Paris; all 346 passengers and crew perish.

The UPC is used for the first time, scanning a pack of Wrigley's gum in Troy, Ohio.

Stephen King publishes his first novel, *Carrie*, and Peter Benchly publishes *Jaws*.

People magazine debuts, with Mia Farrow on the cover.

Lucille Ball's *Here's Lucy* has its series finale.

Happy Days and *The Six Million Dollar Man* first air on ABC.

"Joker" by Steve Miller Band, Barbra Streisand's "The Way We Were," and Gordon Lightfoot's "Sundown" all hit #1 on the Billboard Charts.

Patti Smith releases the first punk-rock single, "Hey Joe."

Mikhail Baryshnikov defects from Russia and joins the American Ballet Theatre.

The Rubik's Cube is invented.

Dungeons & Dragons is released.

Chinatown, The Godfather Part II, Blazing Saddles, and *The Towering Inferno* dominate the box office; *The Sting* wins the Academy Award for best picture.

Hank Aaron ties Babe Ruth's all-time home run record of 714.

Muhammad Ali defeats George Foreman with an eighth round knockout, reclaiming the heavyweight title, in "The Rumble in the Jungle," Kinshasa, Zaire.

Charles Lindbergh, Mama Cass Elliot, Oskar Schindler, Anne Sexton, Duke Ellington, Agnes Moorehead, and Ed Sullivan die.

AND IN NEWFOUNDLAND:

Frank Moores is two years into his term as the second premier of Newfoundland.

There are 162,000 students in the province's school system.

Dorothy Wyatt is the elected mayor of St. John's.

The Come-by-Chance oil refinery is pumping through its first year of production.

And Newfoundland marks twenty-five years of Confederation with Canada with celebrations including the relocation of the *Reach for the Top* championship games to the province's capital city. As the flights, the provincial-level elimination games, play out, the field is narrowed to two teams, Archbishop O'Leary High School of Edmonton, Alberta, the team who had won the last time they participated, two years before, and Gonzaga High School of St. John's, who had never won the championship—no Newfoundland team ever had.

SCENE ONE

ONE GENERATION AFTER

Bill Rowe: It was one generation after Confederation.

Gerry Beresford: The school was great.

Sethu Reddy: It was the twenty-fifth anniversary of Confederation. The championship games were originally scheduled for Regina. We were actually sad [we didn't get to travel somewhere for the game].

Tom Harrington: We rolled our eyes: *There goes our big trip to Regina.*

John Perlin: In 1974 Confederation was still fresh. There were still very, very strong feelings, and that's why the government decided to make such a fuss about it.

Tom Harrington: Gonzaga was a Catholic all-boys school.

Ken Coffey: Until 1972, the uniform was compulsory.

Sethu Reddy: A lot of the teachers were ex-Jesuits. They had spent some time in the seminary and come back to civilian life. I tell people we got a private-school education at public-school prices.

Bill Rowe: The animosities were not forgotten, but the new generation had bigger fish to fry. They were creating a self-confident, knowledgeable generation.

Edward Roberts: In 1974, I was leader of the Liberal Party and Leader of the Opposition. I was elected in White Bay-North in 1966, re-elected in 1971, the more or less tie election that ended with Mr. Smallwood admitting defeat, and I became leader in early '72. It wasn't much of a contest. It wasn't a job many people wanted. It was irrelevant to the election, [PC leader Frank] Moores was going to win, quite handsomely. I held my seat and became Leader of the Opposition.

John Crosbie: And the government Moores led was very much a reform government. We had to be reformers. We had no alternative. After twenty-three years of autocratic rule by the Smallwood Liberals, there was an urgent need for reform on all fronts.[1]

---

[1] John C. Crosbie, *No Holds Barred: My Life in Politics* (Toronto: McClelland & Stewart, 1997), 135.

John Perlin: In 1974, I was director of Cultural Affairs, I was part of the team [organizing the celebrations of the twenty-fifth anniversary of Confederation]. Tom Doyle was the Minister of Recreation; that was before Culture was on the scene. Bob Nutbeam, who was Frank [Moores]'s brother-in-law, was coordinating events.

Pat Bendin: Archbishop O'Leary was a comprehensive high school.

Ihor Gowda: A Catholic school.

Pat Bendin: With several streams.

Ihor Gowda: Co-ed.

Pat Bendin: Fairly big.

Ihor Gowda: About 200-300 students in each grade.

Pat Bendin: A group of four or five students were already practicing [for *Reach for the Top*].

Ihor Gowda: There were try-outs. Our teacher was the coach.

Pat Bendin: Mary-Anne Schepsky.

Ihor Gowda: By the time our team was formed, it was pretty clear, established, who was the lead person in different subject areas.

Pat Bendin: My areas were Canadian history, current events, geography.

Ihor Gowda: I was…science and math were my specialty? Though with Tim Black on the team that seems unlikely.

Tim Black: I had literature, science, visual art, and geography. Brian Mader had music and European history. Our coach was pretty intense about the whole thing. She knew some people working in electronics, and we practiced with a system with lights and buzzers.

Ihor Gowda: You had to know a lot of facts.

Tom Harrington: We were assigned areas of specialization. I was a generalist: history, politics, sports. I was terrible with math, but Gerry was good at that. Peter loved classical music. Sethu knew science. The strength came from all of us. We never had to rely on one person. There was a balance.

Edward Roberts: St. John's was a very much smaller city. Conception Bay South was still the original communities from Topsail to Seal Cove. Torbay and St. Philip's were still essentially rural.

Ken Coffey: Gonzaga's catchment schools included Pius X, Mary Queen of Peace, St. Theresa's/Mundy Pond, St. Joseph's, Outer Cove, Pouch Cove, and Torbay.

Tom Harrington: I grew up on Strawberry Marsh Road. The boys go to Gonzaga, the girls go to Holy Heart.

Gerry Beresford: I came from St. Pat's, which was an unusual route. Most of the guys from St. Pat's went to Brother Rice.

Peter Chafe: Gonzaga was considered by almost everyone in St. John's at the time as being the best Catholic high school and the second-best high school, with Prince of Wales Collegiate Protestant school being better.

Tom Harrington: In terms of the city of St. John's, it was a prominent school. The sports teams were very, very well known. The Gonzaga *Reach for the Top* team had won the provincial championships three years in a row before [1974] and for two years after.

John Perlin: It wasn't a very sophisticated approach [to organizing the twenty-fifth anniversary celebrations].

Bill Rowe: [The restaurant scene and cuisine was] The Starboard Quarter. The John Guy Room. My first date I had with my wife, Penny, was a very, very tony affair: filet mignon; Beaujolais; and it concluded with crème de menthe frappes.

John Perlin: Tom Doyle thought the logo [for Newfoundland's twenty-fifth anniversary as a province] was superb: a fisherman in a dory smoking his pipe upside down.

Edward Roberts: The police were not armed. The prosperity had not come.

John Crosbie: I don't mean to tar all Liberals with the Smallwood brush. During the period I was in Opposition, two of Joey's ministers, Ed Roberts and Bill Rowe—the only ones who had any intelligence to speak of—did try and stand up to Smallwood and to stop some of his worst excesses. There wasn't much they could do but, to give them credit, they used whatever influence they had—which is probably why Joey sabotaged Roberts later, after Ed succeeded him as leader of the Liberals.[2]

Edward Roberts: We knew there was oil.

Ken Coffey: Academics were stressed, as was a concentrated spiritual education, and students were taught to be gentleman, i.e., to walk on the outside of the curb. Gonzaga, like all schools in the province, then went to grade eleven. Grade twelve was introduced in the early 1980s.

Gerry Beresford: I tell you, the first year [at Gonzaga] was rather difficult. Because most of the guys that were there had gone to St. Pius X and known each other right up through. Trying to break into new friendships was difficult in grade ten. A bunch of my buddies were people who didn't go to Pius X. Peter Chafe was from Roncolli.

Peter Chafe: At the school, there were a number of different student groupings including those who lived in the Pius X parish and were from affluent families, those who were bussed in, those who played sports, those who were in the number-one class (a reflection of academic average and

---
[2] Ibid., 110.

specific courses being taken), those who were in the number-two class, and all the other students who primarily were not thinking of going to university. Of course [this] is just one student's perspective, that of a teenager who was an outsider because he was bussed in.

Ken Coffey: There were no bullies. And no allergies.

Tom Harrington: When I was in grade ten, I went to *Reach for the Top* practices, hoping to ingratiate myself. It was almost like being on a varsity team. It was well regarded. We weren't nerds. Trying out was not unusual.

Edward Roberts: The Liberal Party constitution in those days—it may still be the case—in a reaction to Mr. Smallwood, the fact that he was there forever, it was a complicated history, provided that there had to be a leadership convention within two years of an election.

John Perlin: Every province and territory was the guest at a dinner in some part of the province. The first was a disaster. It just wasn't organized. So [Bob] Nutbeam asked Bob Jenkins and me to take over the dinners.

Edward Roberts: I was fine with that. It struck me as reasonable. You're not elected forever. You're not elected until you get thrown out. You're elected for a term that's not greater than two years after the general election.

John Perlin: The plan [for organizing Newfoundland and Labrador's dinners hosting the premiers of the other nine provinces] was that we did pre-visits to each of the host locations and determined who the caterers were and met with them to determine what they wanted to serve and then offered assistance wherever they needed it. And the dinners unfolded.

Edward Roberts. If you win the general election and you want to carry on, there's presumably no problem; if you don't, the party gets the call.

John Perlin: I remember being in Goose Bay with, I think, the premier of Saskatchewan [Allan Blakeney]. We took him fly fishing, and I don't think I've ever seen flies like it. It was awful.

Tom Harrington: Marie Whalen was the librarian and *Reach for the Top* coach, and she had just retired. David Creamer, a young scholastic Jesuit from New Brunswick, took over.

Sethu Reddy: The teachers were very dedicated and put much into extra-curricular activities. I got tremendous benefit from that. It was much more nurturing than a typical public school in Toronto.

Tom Harrington: 1973/1974 was the first year the Gonzaga uniform was no longer required, which most people thought was pretty cool. But David Creamer asked us how we would feel about wearing the uniform, because he thought it would look good and make us feel like a team. The blazers were navy, with a crest [*Diligeus Dominon Deum Tuum*–To the Greater Glory of God].[3]

---

[3] Gonzaga was Jesuit-run, one of the very few such schools in Canada. The Jesuit credo of service translates as "a man for others."

Edward Roberts: Anyway I thought I should carry on. I took the soundings. Everyone was comfortable. Everything was prepared to go ahead. That's what I was doing.

Tom Harrington: David Creamer had a number of strategies. He had the father of a former player build us a set with buzzers.

Edward Roberts: That's ego-centric. There was a lot more happening.

Tom Harrington: Ms. Whalen had somehow acquired sheets and sheets of old *Reach for the Top* questions, but they were disorganized. Somehow he [Creamer] organized them all into games. We had binders of entire *Reach for the Top* games.

Edward Roberts: The Liberal party, which was a rump, there were eight of us in the House of Assembly, maybe nine. We were a rump. Moores had thirty-two or thirty-three of the forty-two seats.

Gerry Beresford: Our routine was every Monday night, which was the night for *Reach for the Top*. We would get together, watch the game, and we would have a practice. And we would have a practice a couple of days a week after school.

Tom Harrington: The Jesuits had a retreat at Hogan's Pond. We would go there on weekends and play games. It was fun, intense; we bonded as a team.

Tim Black: Mary-Anne Schepsky had noticed straight off that they often repeated questions, so she watched and recorded and catalogued. And she added quite a few.

Gerry Beresford: We had question packs: all the questions for the games three years prior to this. Somebody had typed up the questions. Those are questions we would be asked by Father Creamer, Dave Creamer. He would just grab a pack. Some of these repeated themselves.

Tim Black: And there were certain lists all the teams would have memorized: the capitals of all the countries in the world, the capital of all the states, the capitals of all the provinces, the periodic table.

Gerry Beresford: We would play other teams, Holy Heart of Mary. And the year we won, we were the third in four consecutive years of Gonzaga winning [provincially] *Reach for the Top*, so the team from the previous year would come and take us on, as well as the team two years prior.

Tim Black: It was real blood-thirsty competition. There was an alternate, and you could get bumped if you didn't get the numbers. It wasn't like firing the least productive salesman. But we had to complement each other, and be productive.

Gerry Beresford: We competed against other teams, we drilled down through the question packs, we watched the games.

Ken Coffey: The room the *Reach for the Top* team practiced in was small. Father Lloyd Lapinsky showed up one Saturday with a sledgehammer, and he knocked down a wall. That was when I learned it was better to ask for forgiveness than wait for permission.

Gerry Beresford: We started with raise your hands, and about mid-year, the Jesuits actually built a buzzer system. And they built a buzzer system for eight–two teams of four.

Ken Coffey: They had a practice board, so they weren't afraid to ring the buzzer.

Tim Black: We called *Reach for the Top* "press and guess." Our coach didn't want us to guess. We had to have something to say.

Gerry Beresford: We always sat in the same seats. It was always alphabetical in the provincial games: Beresford, Chafe, Harrington, Reddy. So you get used to how tricky your [buzzer is], how much you can depress the buzzer before it's going to trigger. [For the nationals] it was just a different arrangement with the buzzers.

Tim Black: I had a habit, if I didn't know the answer but the question was about a person, of saying Archibald MacLeish [American poet]. She snuck in some questions where the answer *was* Archibald MacLeish. So I learned not to do that.

Gerry Beresford: I don't know why we changed our seating in the nationals. I can't remember that. But I was always closest to the moderator, and in the national finals I was furthest away. I can't remember why we did that. It might have been because they didn't want me to get too used to one particular buzzer.

Tim Black: If you pressed the button you must have something to say.

Sethu Reddy: It also taught us something about the timing. The right time to buzz. As the question is read each word is potentially another clue.

Gerry Beresford: The Jesuits gave us the same buzzer system that was on the provincials. In the national finals [*Reach for the Top*] changed the buzzers. They didn't want to give the Newfoundland team an advantage. It was a new buzzer system that they put into place for the nationals.

Edward Roberts: Politics was much more straightforward.

Bill Rowe: Frank Moores defeated Joey.

Edward Roberts: I was Leader of the Opposition. There were NDP [party] members but nobody'd been elected. [Premier] Frank [Moores] was an interesting fellow. No personal animosity between us.

Bill Rowe: A breath of fresh air. Frank Moores was laid back.

Edward Roberts: People thought he was lazy and lackadaisical. He knew what he wanted. He ran his cabinet, when he said jump, they jumped.

Bill Rowe: Every thinking person, in St. John's especially, wanted Joey out. And Joey Smallwood—I was in the House and caucus and government with Smallwood, and there was a lot about Joey I couldn't stand, but there was something I could stand, I could stand a lot of, and that was, as a man who had no university education himself, who was an autodidact, self-educated, he was a man who was absolutely devoted to the university and all the attributes of the university and making sure that every Newfoundlander and Labradorian had a chance to go to the university.

Edward Roberts: The Confederation Building was one building. Mr. [Pierre] Trudeau was Prime Minister.

Bill Rowe: Scholarships were created. They were coming out of our ears.

Edward Roberts: Ray Guy [then a regular columnist with *The Evening Telegram*] was a must-read. Brilliant, brilliant, stuff.

Bill Rowe: When you first asked me about this I said I was away; I spent the year in the south of France with my family. But I've since realized that the reason I was away was the same reason for the *Reach for the Top* team doing what they did. Newfoundland at the time was going through an Elizabethan Age, there was a renaissance going on. A lot of the people in 1974 who were thriving were part of that uprising in learning, culture, knowledge, you name it.

Peter Chafe: Unlike most people I hear talking about high school, for me my two years at Gonzaga were golden years; it was an awakening for me.

Bill Rowe: In those days, we weren't riding so high economically as we are now; there was also a bit of defensiveness about being a Newfoundlander, because morons on the mainland looked down their noses at the Newfoundland accent and handouts. There was a defensiveness added to the self-confidence which added to the Newfoundland Renaissance. The *Reach for the Top* team, it seems to me, were tip of the iceberg, youngsters who seemed supremely confident they could compete with anybody. They were proud to be Newfoundlanders, the little principality here, the tribe of Newfoundlanders and Labradorians, it all came together. A symbol of what was happening.

Peter Chafe: Coming from a poorer area, I knew very little about the world and the people in it. But within a couple of months, my two best friends were an Indian (Sethu Reddy) and a Filipino (Michael Bautista). We were a tight group, focused on achieving academic excellence.

Ken Coffey: The schools were organized into different "flights" and played off each other with winners moving up, like in the hockey playoffs.

Tom Harrington: At the time [getting to the national championship] was somewhat of an achievement. We were grade eleven. Newfoundlanders in national competitions, outside of the Faulkners,[4] there weren't a lot of success stories. It was a big deal.

Gerry Beresford: What do I remember about the game? I remember so much. The place was packed. You had to have a ticket to get into the studio. There were so many people that showed up they had to have another room for people to watch it in.

---

[4] George Faulkner and Alex Faulkner (born 1933 and 1936, respectively, in Bishop's Falls) were the first professional hockey players from Newfoundland and Labrador.

SCENE TWO

THIS IS THE GAME OF THE YEAR

July 5, 1974
The CBC-TV studio at 95 University Avenue in St. John's:

The images are in black & white. The tail end of the Here & Now *theme plays, as side-by-side outlines of Newfoundland and Labrador, scaled to about the same size, are projected on the screen.*

Bob Cole: (*Introducing the two teams*) ...Tim Black, Brian Mader, Pat Bendin, and Ihor Gowda from Archbishop O'Leary High School in Edmonton, Alberta.

Ihor Gowda: [At our school] there was a big tradition with *Reach for the Top*.

Tim Black: The city organized it so the school had a team every two years.

Ihor Gowda: Two years before, our team had won the national championships.

Tim Black: There was that hanging over our heads.

Bob Cole: They meet Peter Chafe, Sethu Reddy, Tom Harrington, and Gerry Beresford from Gonzaga High School in St. John's, Newfoundland, in the Championship Game of the National Playoffs of *Reach for the Top*.

The Alberta team are individually dressed in casual slacks and shirts with flared collars; Pat Bendin wears a V-neck sweater. The Gonzaga team wears grey pants, white shirts, and their blue, crested school blazers. Peter Chafe and Gerry Beresford sport bow-ties, and Beresford also has a lucky charm on a chain, a Viking,[1] given to him by a friend.

Gerry Beresford: We won the provincial championship in June. Sethu and Peter both chose to forego writing the public exams. Tom and I, being not as smart as Peter and Sethu, chose to write all our publics. Peter and Sethu just worked like slaves on *Reach for the Top*. Worked and worked and worked. We practiced most every day leading up to the tournament [starting June 29, with the final game July 5].

Tim Black: Our team was Ihor—and everybody else. He has a mind like a steel trap. His memory...After high school he went to Vegas and counted cards. He read the *World Book Encyclopedia* twice. Ihor got twice the points of anybody else.

Cut to audience, applauding, a Jesuit priest among them.

---

1 Gonzaga's sports teams are called The Vikings.

We see the Reach for the Top *opening montage and theme.*

Sethu Reddy: Going into the game, I think we were at least one or two years younger than everyone else.

Ihor Gowda: I remember we were pretty confident. I won't say cocky. But we thought we were going to win.

Sethu Reddy: We expected to lose. The teams from Northern Ontario and Alberta were consistently very strong, and for them there was a lot of pressure. For us it was a pleasant surprise to get to the final. We enjoyed the game.

Peter Chafe: We considered ourselves fortunate every time we beat another province, partly because they were "the mainland," but also because they were one or two years older than us, being in grades twelve or thirteen. Newfoundland was unique in having grade eleven as the last grade of high school.

Tim Black: I remember distinctly, on the way up to the nationals, all through the provincials, we were really cocky, we were the only team that had to be bleeped, we were very rude. We never less than doubled the score.

Ihor Gowda: I remember there was somebody on the Saskatchewan team, a rebellious type, he was bookmaking, with a point spread, and letting people bet. We were forty point favourites, just based on who we had played earlier and by how much we had won.

Brian Mader: We had Ihor Gowda.

Tim Black: But it was a raucous crowd. That rattled us.

Pat Bendin: I remember a very enthusiastic audience. It was a big deal.

Tom Harrington: It was not a big studio. Sometimes the noise level was such Bill Guest couldn't ask a question.

Tim Black: It was intense.

Tom Harrington: It was to the rafters. It was like a hockey game. The atmosphere was electric.

Bill Rowe: They were going for it. They went for it.

Pat Bendin: We had not prepared for that game with as much discipline as we had; usually we met the night before to talk about our roles, what we knew about the other team. But we were off enjoying ourselves.

Sethu Reddy: Looking back after forty years, I see we were teenagers.

Peter Chafe: The thing that I remember most about the championship game was how calm I was.

Pat Bendin: Right off the bat, we were not quite on.

Sethu Reddy: We were buzzing too quickly.

Peter Chafe: A calmness that I had before, during and after every game. I felt no stress or anxiety, no fear. I guess in my mind, still being an outsider, I had nothing to lose. I wish that I could say that this tranquility was always part of my nature, before and after *Reach for the Top*, but that was not the case, as many people will attest, especially those who heard me give extremely nervous presentations and speeches throughout my life.

Cut to Bob Cole, behind a podium. He wears a light shirt and jacket and wide striped tie. Behind him is a chart showing the progression of winning teams, now with ALTA linked to NFLD. A graphic of Cabot Tower can be seen at its centre.

Bob Cole: Hello again, everyone, I'm Bob Cole, your host in St. John's, Newfoundland, for the championship game today for the *Reach for the Top* playoffs this year. And as you can see from the white board behind me, a lot of great teams have been eliminated. We're down to two now. One from Alberta, and one from Newfoundland. And here with the championship game, is your quizmaster, from Winnipeg, Manitoba, Bill Guest.

Tom Harrington: He was the Danny Gallivan[2] of *Reach for the Top*. He was the voice.

Bill Guest: (*Wearing a dark shirt and jacket, patterned tie and*

---

2 Gallivan, the legendary sportscaster, spent more than three decades calling games for *Hockey Night in Canada*.

glasses, he stands behind a podium with stylized Reach for the Top *logo, and a mic. He holds a pen in his left hand.*) Thank you, Bob, very much. Hello again, everybody, nice to be back with you for a very exciting game. This is the game of the year. When this half hour is up, as Bob says, one of these two exceptionally fine teams will be the national champions here in Canada, the cream of the crop, and which will it be? Well even our fine judges don't know the answer to that question, but they will be listening to the answers to all of the questions that are asked tonight. Here's Pat O'Flaherty first of all (*applause*). Pat is an associate professor of English at Memorial University in St. John's, and one of the best boosters Newfoundland has ever had. Next to Pat we find this gentleman, who is another distinguished educator, Bob Curies is from Montreal, ladies and gentlemen. He teaches at Dawson College in Montreal, and he's anxious to see the outcome of today's game. And our chief adjudicator is another outstanding educator, from Alberta. This is Gene Balay, ladies and gentlemen, a supervisor of English at the Alberta Correspondence School. Well, I hope all of your decisions are very easy ones today, gentlemen.

SCENE THREE

"WELL, SIRS, LET'S CHECK THE SCORES."

Bill Guest: Let's begin with this first question. Now, and this takes us into the area of sports. Good luck with this ten-pointer. And it's winners we're after this time. Which NHL team won the Stanley Cup—

Ihor Gowda buzzes.

Bill Guest: Uh, Ihor.

Ihor Gowda: The Philadelphia Flyers.

Bill Guest: That's not right. The question is Newfoundland's. (*Sethu lifts and flexes his hands, a characteristic gesture he will repeat throughout the game.*) Which NHL team won the Stanley Cup in the 1971-1972 season?

Tom Harrington buzzes.

Bill Guest: Which was it, Tom?

Tom Harrington: Boston.

Bill Guest: That's correct.

Gonzaga 10 points.

Pat Bendin: I remember the flow of the game. We started off badly. We fell behind.

Ihor Gowda: Two things happened. We were thrown by the intensity of the hometown crowd. The first time Newfoundland answered a question the crowd exploded.

Tom Harrington: They would erupt like we scored a goal in the Stanley Cup.

Ihor Gowda: We were, not to say intimidated, but it was a shock, it tightened us up.

Bill Guest: Try this. In 1972 who won—

Brian Mader buzzes.

Bill Guest: Yes, Brian?

Brian Mader: Miami.

Bill Guest: That will not do. Newfoundland, in 1972 who won the world amateur ice hockey championship.

Tom Harrington buzzes.

Bill Guest: Who was that, Tom?

Tom Harrington: Czechoslovakia.

Bill Guest: That is right for ten points.

Gonzaga 20.

Pat Bendin: Our leader was Ihor Gowda, and it seemed to me he was being much more differential to us than usual. I was surprised.

Ihor Gowda: And we were never really established. We were falling behind, and that threw us even further into a loop.

Bill Guest: Now in the same year, 1972, who was the world Grand Prix champion?

Gerry Beresford buzzes.

Bill Guest: Who was that, Gerry?

Gerry has no answer. Ihor Gowda buzzes.

Bill Guest: You know, Ihor?

Ihor Gowda: Jackie Stewart.

Bill Guest: No, it was Emerson Fittipaldi of Brazil. He drove a Lotus Ford. Now, and a year later in 1973, who was declared the Canadian Open golf champion?

Gerry Beresford buzzes.

Bill Guest: Gerry?

Gerry Beresford: *(answer is unclear)*

Bill Guest: That is not right.

Brian Mader buzzes.

Bill Guest: Do you know, Brian?

Brian Mader: Dave Brewer?

Bill Guest: It was Tom Weiskopf of the USA. Well, this next question is a scramble, and it's worth forty-five points. Try this, please, anyone. How many articles are there in one gross?

Gerry Beresford buzzes.

Bill Guest: How many, Gerry?

Gerry Beresford: Forty-four.

Bill Guest: That is right.

Gonzaga 25.

The crowd applauds so loudly they drown out something Bill Guest says about Newfoundland's score.

Bill Guest: Now Newfoundland, we have more here, more about weights and measures. How many gills are there in one quart? How many gills, Newfoundland?

All consult. Gerry Beresford buzzes.

Gerry Beresford: Thirty-two.

Bill Guest: Pardon?

Gerry Beresford: Thirty-two.

Bill Guest: The answer is eight. How many quarts are there in four gallons?

Gerry Beresford buzzes.

Bill Guest: Gerry?

Gerry Beresford: Sixteen.

Bill Guest: Sixteen. How many feet are there in ten miles?

Gerry Beresford buzzes.

Bill Guest: Gerry?

Gerry Beresford: Fifty-two thousand, (*hesitates a second, working out the number, uses his hand for emphasis*) eight hundred.

Bill Guest: Right on. And how many acres are there in ten square miles?

Gerry Beresford buzzes.

Bill Guest: Gerry?

Gerry Beresford: Six thousand four hundred.

Bill Guest: Yes, six thousand four hundred.

Peter Chafe: We were a balanced team and we mostly respected each other's categories, allowing the person responsible to take the question.

Bill Guest: Well, (*turns a page*) you did well with weights and measures, let's see what you know about singers. This is an open question for both teams, what outstanding singer have we here? Listen please.

Harry Nilsson's "Are You Sleeping?" plays.

Brian Mader buzzes.

Bill Guest: All right, Brian.

Brian Mader: Nat King Cole.

Bill Guest: That's not right, Brian.

Gonzaga 55 points.

Song continues. Tom Harrington buzzes.

Bill Guest: OK, Tom?

Tom Harrington: Neil Diamond?

Bill Guest: No, the answer is Nilsson, "Are You Sleeping?" That was Nilsson. Now, for ten points, who is this? Listen carefully.

Gordon Lightfoot's "Alberta Bound" plays. Pat Bendin buzzes.

Bill Guest: Pat?

Pat Bendin: Glen Campbell.

Bill Guest: No, it is not.

Tom Harrington buzzes.

Bill Guest: Tom?

Tom Harrington: Gordon Lightfoot?

Bill Guest: Yes, it's Gordon Lightfoot, and he was singing

"Alberta Bound," Pat.

Tom Harrington rubs his hands with a cloth—his characteristic gesture.

Tom Harrington: I was sixteen, but I had been singing on stage and TV since I was six. We had a family group, The Sanderlings. I was on *The Tommy Hunter Show*. But I have clammy hands. They could slip off the buzzer. I had a little towel in all the games.

Gonzaga 65.

Bill Guest: Here's the next one. I have the distinct feeling you'll get this one. Listen carefully please.

Elvis Presley's "Hound Dog" plays. Pat Bendin buzzes.

Bill Guest: Yes, Pat?

Pat Bendin: Elvis Presley.

Bill Guest: That's who it is, didn't take too long to get the hound dog. And here's, ah, here's um, here's a philosophical song, but what group is it? What group this time? Listen.

The Rolling Stones' "You Can't Always Get What You Want" plays. Ihor Gowda buzzes.

Bill Guest: All right, Ihor.

Ihor Gowda: The Rolling Stones.

Bill Guest: Yes. The Rolling Stones is right.

Alberta 20
Gonzaga 65

Bill Guest: Now, let's have a Who Am I? question here. And this is worth forty points on the first clue as you know. Try this. I was born in 1659 in London, England, and although I started a career as a merchant, I soon became known as a pamphleteer and a political journalist.

Gerry Beresford buzzes.

Bill Guest: Try it, Gerry.

Gerry Beresford: Voltaire.

Bill Guest: That's not right. (*Gerry Beresford bows his head to the desktop.*) The last part of the clue for Alberta. My most famous pamphlet called *The Shortest Day, The Shortest Way With Dissenters,* earned me a sentence in prison, and some time in the pillory as well. Who am I, do you know, anyone in Alberta?

Brian Mader buzzes.

Bill Guest: Yes, Brian?

Brian Mader: (*hesitates, makes a frustrated gesture*) Locke.

Bill Guest: That is not right. Second clue. Both teams go for this now. I became one of the first English writers of novels, using realism with great effect—

Peter Chafe buzzes.

Bill Guest: Yes, Peter?

Peter Chafe: John Bunyan.

Bill Guest: That's not right. The last part of this clue for Alberta now, for example, one of my works is a fictitious history purporting to be the authentic account of a resident of London during the year of the Great Plague. Who am I? Do you know, Alberta?

Ihor Gowda buzzes.

Bill Guest: Ihor?

Ihor Gowda: Richardson?

Bill Guest: No. Next clue for twenty points: Kim Novak starred in a movie based on one of my novels called *The Fortunes and Misfortunes of Moll Flanders*.

Pat Bendin buzzes.

Bill Guest: Who am I, Pat?

Pat Bendin: Hardy?

Bill Guest: No, do you know, Newfoundland?

Sethu Reddy buzzes.

Bill Guest: Sethu?

Sethu Reddy: Daniel Dafoe.

Bill Guest: That's who it is. (*Huge cheer from the audience. Sethu flexes his hands.*)

Alberta 20
Gonzaga 85

Bill Guest: (*turning another page*) Well, here's a, here's another, here's another open question, this one is about battles. I'm going to name the war, you tell me the, who the combatants were, if you can. Here's the first one. Who were the two leaders in the civil war in England—

Brian Mader buzzes.

Bill Guest: Yes, Brian?

Brian Mader: Richard Cromwell and King Charles—

Bill Guest: No, that's a different—I'll repeat this for Newfoundland, who were the two leaders in the civil war in England 1642-46. Your question now.

Peter Chafe buzzes.

Bill Guest: Go ahead, Peter.

Peter Chafe: Oliver Cromwell and Charles the First.

Alberta 20
Gonzaga 95

Bill Guest: That's it. Yes. All right. Now it's open remember, it's open, what two countries were involved in the One Hundred Years War, 13—

Gerry Beresford buzzes.

Bill Guest: Yes, Gerry.

Gerry Beresford: England and France?

Bill Guest: That's correct, yes, 1338 to 1450.

Alberta 20
Gonzaga 105

Bill Guest: What were the two principle countries involved in the War of 1812?

Gerry Beresford buzzes.

Bill Guest: What two, Gerry?

Gerry Beresford: The United States and Britain.

Bill Guest: Fine, ok.

Alberta 20
Newfoundland 115.

Bill Guest: And it was between 431 and 404 BC—

Gerry Beresford buzzes.

Bill Guest: Yes, Gerry?

Gerry Beresford: Um, Carthage and Rome.

Bill Guest: No, that won't do. This question for Alberta now. It was between 431 and 404 BC, what city states opposed one another in the Peloponnesian War?

Brian Mader buzzes.

Bill Guest: Your answer please, Brian?

Brian Mader: Athens and Sparta.

Bill Guest: That's what we want for that, yes. Well these next forty-five points could be yours if you get the scramble (*turning page*). Good luck with this. In the binary representation of numbers, how many different kinds of digits are used?

Gerry Beresford buzzes.

Bill Guest: How many, Gerry?

Gerry Beresford: Two.

Bill Guest: Right on.

Gerry Beresford: The other thing about the game and the way we operated—in *Reach for the Top* there were open questions and there were scramble questions. And with scramble questions, if you got the first answer the rest of the questions were yours. And the way we worked, whoever got the scramble—you could consult in a scramble—they were the people that subsequently answered the questions that followed. The scramble came and it was how many numbers in a bi- and I buzzed, of course it was two, and I got the scramble. The next four questions were all about mod math.

Alberta 30
Newfoundland 120

Tom Harrington folds a cloth

Bill Guest: All right, Newfoundland. We have more about numbers here and the way we use them. You may use your pencils on these, Newfoundland, if you wish. Please convert these numbers to a decimal number, that is one having base ten. All right, try this, here's the first. Two one base three. What's the answer?

Gerry Beresford buzzes.

Bill Guest: Gerry Beresford.

Gerry Beresford: Three.

Bill Guest: That's not right. The answer is seven.

Gerry Beresford: Mod math is something we never learned. [The Alberta team] were grade twelve, grade thirteen; we didn't learn mod math until first year university. We didn't know how [mod math] worked, because we hadn't learned it.

Bill Guest: Try this: two three base four.

Sethu Reddy seems to try the buzzer, but it doesn't sound. Gerry Beresford buzzes.

Bill Guest: The answer, Gerry?

Gerry Beresford: Seventeen.

Bill Guest: The answer is eleven. One one base five.

Peter Chafe buzzes.

Bill Guest: Peter?

Peter Chafe: Two.

Bill Guest: That's not right. The answer is six. And the final one is three five base six.

Gerry Beresford buzzes.

Bill Guest: The answer, Gerry?

Gerry Beresford: Seventeen.

Bill Guest: The answer is twenty-three. (*Gerry makes a disgusted gesture with his pencil.*)

Gerry Beresford: So while we got the scramble, we got none of the subsequent answers. So we got five points for the scramble, and zero points thereafter. But, if we hadn't gotten the scramble—[the Alberta team] knew every single answer. I could hear the frustration above my head, as we were throwing out answers that meant nothing to anybody. These guys were just tearing their hair out because it would have been an easy forty points for them.

Bill Guest: Well here come a few short snappers for a change. Try these, please, anyone. Who was thrown into a lion's den for breaking—

Peter Chafe buzzes.

Bill Guest: Yes, Peter?

Peter Chafe: Daniel.

Bill Guest: That's right, yes. According to the Bible, who was supposedly swallowed by a whale?

Peter Chafe buzzes.

Bill Guest: Who was that, Peter?

Peter Chafe: Jonah.

Bill Guest: Yes. This one for ten points, name the Portuguese explorer who was the first man—

Pat Bendin buzzes.

Bill Guest: Yes?

Pat Bendin: Corte Real.

Bill Guest: No, the question is Newfoundland's, the Portuguese explorer who was the first man to sail around the Cape of Good Hope to India.

Sethu Reddy buzzes.

Bill Guest: Sethu?

Sethu Reddy: Vasco da Gama.

Bill Guest: That's who it was, yes. Who wrote *The Study in Scarlet*?

Tim Black buzzes.

Bill Guest: Who did that, Tim?

Tim Black scratches his head and seems to say Conner Doyle.

Bill Guest: Newfoundland, please, anyone there?

Gerry Beresford buzzes.

Bill Guest: Gerry?

Gerry Beresford: Conan Doyle.

Alberta 30
Newfoundland 160

Bill Guest: That's right. Who wrote *Tender is the Night*? Who wrote that?

Ihor Gowda buzzes.

Bill Guest: Ihor?

Ihor Gowda: Daniel DaFoe?

Bill Guest: I beg your pardon?

Tom Harrington buzzes.

Bill Guest: Tom, go ahead.

Tom Harrington: F. Scott Fitzgerald.

Bill Guest: It was Scott Fitzgerald, yeah. What was the first name of Scott Fitzgerald's wife, anyone?

Ihor Gowda buzzes.

Bill Guest: Ihor?

Ihor Gowda: Zelda.

Bill Guest: That's right. Zelda. What is the capital of the Dominican Republic?

Ihor Gowda buzzes.

Bill Guest: Ihor?

Ihor Gowda: Santo Domingo.

Bill Guest: That's right. What great explorer is said to be buried in the cathedral of—

Gerry Beresford buzzes.

Bill Guest: Yes, Gerry?

Gerry Beresford: Ah …

Alberta 45
Newfoundland 170

Bill Guest: Try it please, I'll finish it Alberta, buried in the cathedral of Santo Domingo—

Tim Black buzzes.

Bill Guest: Who is that?

Tim Black: Columbus.

Bill Guest: Columbus is right.

Tim Black: Everything was trivial, the result of rote learning. They did have some puzzles, but almost everything was recall. If you have that kind of recall you're probably pretty smart anyway, an overachiever.

Bill Guest: And finally, what kind of creature is kept in an a—

Gerry Beresford buzzes.

Gerry Beresford: The game itself, there was a time in the game…to go back to the provincials, Bob Cole, really good guy, but when you buzzed with Bob Cole he tended to finish the sentence. He couldn't stop. When you buzzed with Bill Guest, in the middle of a syllable, Bill Guest stopped cold.

Bill Guest: (*Stops cold.*)

Gerry Beresford: He was a great moderator.

Bill Guest: (*Waits.*)

Gerry Beresford: And I remember in the game, there was a question, "What lives in an a—" and I buzzed as I always do. Quick with the trigger but not with the answers sometimes. And he stopped on the letter a.

Bill Guest: A—

Gerry Beresford: He looked at me, I'll never forget him looking at me, and I looked at him and I said...

Bill Guest: Gerry?

Gerry Beresford: Bird.

Gerry Beresford: "A bird." I don't know where that came from. I have absolutely no idea where the word *bird* came from.

Bill Guest: Yes, an aviary, that's right.

Gerry Beresford: The question was "What lives in an aviary?" I think I would have been in fourth year university before I knew what an aviary was.

Gerry adjusts his glasses and turns away for a moment.

Tom Harrington: Gerry expresses how we all felt. He was jumping in a lot. We killed everyone in the flights. We could have 580 points a game, have 500 to 150 or 230. Enormous victories.

Alberta 55
Newfoundland 175

Bill Guest: Well, sirs, let's check the scores. Alberta has fifty-five points and Newfoundland is leading here with 175. (*This changes to 185 as soon as he says this.*) We'll get on with this week's final contest on *Reach for the Top* after we break for these important messages.

The screen shows a Canada vs USSR static image of crossed, flagged hockey sticks. A voiceover explains that CBC will carry four games in the Team Canada versus USSR hockey series on its entire television network.

SCENE FOUR

THAT WAS WHEN WE LOST THE GAME

[TAKE 1]

Edward Roberts: To set the political scene, I hadn't won the election, I'd lost it. The Liberals lost, quite disastrously, and I was leader, so I took the responsibility. We lost a by-election in the summer of '72.

The Opposition leader was not very much in the public eye. Moores was the new Premier. The Liberal rule of twenty-two years had ended, all that stuff. The Labrador linerboard mill, Come-by-Chance, this was what political dialogue was about. Frank was finding his way, make your own judgment, on what he found and how he found it.
There was no particular interest in the leader of the Liberal party, period.

We had a by-election in the fall of '73. Roy Cheeseman decided to run in Hermitage in the '72 election for Frank, and got elected. *You* would have been elected, *I* would have been elected, running for the Tories in Hermitage in 1972. And he became Fisheries Minister.

And after a year or so, for whatever reason, he wanted to leave elected politics, and he did. He resigned as the member for Hermitage.

So there was a by-election, and we threw everything we had into it. We had nothing better to do, and we won. Roger Simmons was elected.

1974 came along, and the Liberal executive, with my full consent and co-operation and support, scheduled a leadership convention. And at some point Mr. Smallwood—he and I had a distant relationship, he disappeared to Florida after the election in '72, he was back and forth, he was around—he rang me one day, would I come to see him? And I said, sure.

I got in the car, and I went over to Roche's Line. And we spent an hour or so together, and the gist of his scheme was that Moores was not doing well as premier. This was what Mr. Smallwood was hearing. I don't think there was any poll or anything like that. It may have been what he wanted to hear. Who knows?

Well, I agree, people are beginning to realize that Frank is not the answer to everything. Well, he said, you know, I still have a lot of friends around.

I agreed. He was probably more popular than when he lost in

'71 and left a mess to us in '72.

And he eventually came to the point: he said what I should do was, when the election came, form a coalition with him. I should step down as leader and let him succeed to the leadership, return, and that he and I jointly would select candidates, and that when the election was over—he had no doubt, Mr. Smallwood, whatever else he was he was a salesman, and he may have believed what he was saying—whenever the election was over, whichever of us had the more, greater number of candidates would become the premier.

He said think about it.

I said I don't really have to think about that. That just isn't workable. The discussion became heated, and it ended there. I said, now look, I'm the leader, I took responsibility for your defeat, we've turned things around. Hermitage is a good sign. There won't be an election for a year or so. I think we're going to go on.

He wasn't happy with the decision, but we didn't come to fisticuffs. He went his way and I went mine.

And then I began to hear he was interested in running for the leadership. He knew the leadership was coming up. I should stand aside, and he would run and all would be well again, like 1952. He began gathering his friends together, people who'd supported him for years. He put together a group, and they weren't insubstantial.

And he ran.

I didn't not run.

He was surprised.

And at the end of the day, I beat him. It took two ballots. But it was quite decisive. Which made me one of two men in history to beat Mr. Smallwood in an election. The other was Herman Quinton in 1932.

Anyway we had it out. So that was that. I was back as leader. I had a mandate for the next election.

SCENE FIVE

THAT WAS WHEN WE LOST THE GAME
[TAKE 2]

OR

AND THEN THE BUZZER WENT, AND I LEAPT UP

Bob Cole: (*Voice over*) Now for more in our championship game, here's Bill Guest.

Bill Guest: Thank you, Bob, very much, thank you. And it's quite a contest, this one, and teams we're moving to our assigned questions here now. These questions are about lakes in Canada. I hope you know our lakes well. I'll give you the name of the lake, and you name the province or the territory in which that lake [is located]. Now, Tim Black, you're first with this assigned question for ten points. In which province is Lake Claire?

Split screen shows Tim Black and Peter Chafe.

Bill Guest: Lake—

Tim Black: Manitoba.

Bill Guest: That is not right. For five points, Peter, do you know?

Peter Chafe: Ontario.

Bill Guest: The answer happens to be Alberta. (*Tim Black laughs; everyone laughs.*) Okay, try this, Peter Chafe. Peter Chafe, this is your question. Where is Lake, Lake Nipigon?

Peter Chafe: Ontario.

Bill Guest: In Ontario, yes. All right (*split screen moving to Brian Mader and Tom Harrington*), for ten points now, Brian Mader, your turn. In what province do we find Lake Melville?

Brian Mader: Ontario.

Bill Guest: That is not right. Do you know, Tom?

Tom Harrington: Newfoundland and Labrador.

Bill Guest: Now that's fine, okay, good answer for that for five points. Now, Tom, this is yours. How about Lake Barber?

Tom Harrington: Ah, Nova Scotia?

Bill Guest: Nova Scotia's the answer. Now for ten points (*split screen shifts to Pat Bendin and Sethu Reddy*). Pat Bendin, where do we find Lake Kootenay?

Pat Bendin: British Columbia.

Bill Guest: That is right on, for ten points. And Sethu Reddy, this is yours. Where do we find Great Bear Lake?

Sethu Reddy: (*pause*) Yukon.

Bill Guest: Ah, that will not do. Pat Bendin?

Pat Bendin: (*Overlapping*) Northwest Territories.

Bill Guest: Yes, that's more like it, for five points. (*Split screen shows Ihor Gowda and Gerry Beresford.*) And Ihor Gowda, this is yours. In what province do we find Lac la Ronge? Lac la Ronge?

Ihor Gowda: Quebec?

Bill Guest: That's not right, perhaps Gerry?

Gerry Beresford: New Brunswick?

Bill Guest: The answer is Saskatchewan, for Lac la Ronge. And here's the last one for you, Gerry Beresford. Lake Mistassini is in what province?

Gerry Beresford: Quebec.

Bill Guest: That is right on for ten points, yeah. Okay. Now teams if, if you like still life, still life paintings (*turns page*) I think you'll like what we have here now, because we want you to identify the artist who painted the still life you're about to see. First of all this one on your monitor right now for ten points (*image of* Still Life Apples Grapes Pear *by James*

Peale, sound of buzzer). Yes, Tim Black?

Tim Black: Murillo.

Bill Guest: That's not right. You know, Peter?

Peter Chafe: Chardin?

Bill Guest: James Peale painted that fruit. Now who saw this table—(*image of Paul Cézanne's* Kitchen Table (Still-Life with Basket), *buzzer*) yes, Tim?

Tim Black: Cézanne.

Bill Guest: You're right, you got it, Cézanne, Cézanne for, for ten points, that was the *Kitchen Table*. That came up pretty fast (*image of Arshile Gorky's* Landscape Table *appears, buzzer*). All right Tim?

Tim Black: Klee?

Bill Guest: No, that isn't right. Newfoundland, anyone there know?

Peter Chafe buzzes.

Bill Guest: Peter?

Peter Chafe: Picasso.

Bill Guest: No, that isn't right. Arshile Gorky painted the

Landscape Table. And finally who put these plum blossoms (*image of Henri Matisse's* Plum Blossoms, Green Background *appears*)—

Peter Chafe buzzes.

Bill Guest: Peter?

Peter Chafe: Matisse.

Bill Guest: That's right. Henri Matisse, quite right. Well, we have a few facts about Canada, I hope you know your facts (*turning pages*). Now I have a question, a forty-five-point team question. How many provinces in Canada have a smaller population than the city of Toronto?

Pat Bendin buzzes.

Bill Guest: Pat?

Pat Bendin: One.

Bill Guest: That's not right. Do you know, Newfoundland?

Peter Chafe buzzes.

Bill Guest: Peter?

Peter Chafe: Three.

Bill Guest: The answer is eight. (*Peter reacts, can you believe* *that?*) Only Quebec and Ontario have larger populations. All right (*turns more pages*), here's another thirty-five-point team question for you. Scramble for this one. Which continent contains over forty countries?

Alberta 80
Newfoundland 220

Ihor Gowda buzzes.

Bill Guest: Which is that, Ihor?

Ihor Gowda: Africa.

Bill Guest: That's right. Second part of this now for the Alberta team.

Alberta 85

Bill Guest: Now, Alberta, now naturally this is about Africa and its places (*team looks towards each other*). What is the name of the country that is surrounded by South Africa and was formerly called Basutoland? What's the name of it?

Pat Bendin buzzes.

Bill Guest: Pat?

Pat Bendin: Botswana?

Bill Guest: Lesotho is the answer. Which three African

countries have the Atlas mountains in them? You must have the three of them.

Alberta consults. Brian Mader buzzes.

Bill Guest: Okay, Brian.

Brian Mader: Algeria, Morocco, and Niger.

Bill Guest: Ah, no, sorry: Algeria, Morocco, and Tunisia. And what is the name of the lake that's found between Malawi and Tanzania? Name of the lake, anyone know? Try it please, Brian.

Brian Mader: Lake Victoria.

Bill Guest: Lake Nyasa is the answer to that.

Bill Guest: More geography, in the form of a What Country Am I? this time. Both teams go to work on this one. For forty points, I'm a limited monarchy with a queen, a member of the UN and NATO, and I joined the European Economic Community—

Gerry Beresford buzzes.

Bill Guest: Yes, Gerry,

Gerry Beresford: Luxembourg.

Bill Guest: That's not right. I joined the European Economic

Community in 1973—

Brian Mader buzzes.

Bill Guest: Brian?

Brian Mader: The Netherlands.

Bill Guest: That's not right. Second clue for thirty points.

Brian Mader buzzes.

Bill Guest: Try it, Brian.

Brian Mader: Denmark.

Bill Guest: That's what it is, Denmark. Yes, indeed, for thirty points. Good for you. Okay, you didn't need that second clue. Now we're going to listen to some music here for a change. We want you to as usual identify the composers of these rhapsodies, overtures, and symphonies. Here's the first. Who composed this, please?

Franz Liszt's "Hungarian Rhapsody No. 2 in C-sharp minor" plays.

Alberta 115
Newfoundland 220

Brian Mader buzzes.

Bill Guest: Brian Mader.

Brian Mader: Tchaikovsky.

Bill Guest: That's not right. More for Newfoundland on this one.

Sethu Reddy buzzes.

Bill Guest: Sethu.

Sethu Reddy: Borodin.

Bill Guest: Franz Liszt is the answer. That was the "Hungarian Rhapsody No. 2." Next composer: who composed this?

Pyotr Ilyich Tchaikovsky's "The Year 1812, festival overture in Eb major, Op. 49" (also known as the "1812 Overture") plays. Brian Mader buzzes. Sethu Reddy buzzes almost the same time.

Bill Guest: Brian?

Brain Mader: Wagner.

Bill Guest: That's not right. Sethu?

Sethu Reddy: Mozart.

Bill Guest: It is Tchaikovsky this time, his "1812 Overture." Now this is not second, fourth, or sixth but somebody's fifth symphony, but whose?

Brian Mader buzzes before the sound cue.

Bill Guest: Listen, Brian.

The opening of Ludwig Van Beethoven's "Fifth Symphony in C Minor" plays.

Brian Mader: Beethoven.

Bill Guest: That's what it is. (*Brian Mader looks relieved.*) Beethoven, yes. And I wonder if you recognize this music. The composer please, anyone?

Alberta 125
Newfoundland 220

Franz Shubert's "Symphony No. 8 in B minor, D" (also known as the "Unfinished Symphony") plays. Brian Mader buzzes.

Bill Guest: Brian Mader.

Brian Mader: Schubert.

Alberta 135
Newfoundland 220

Bill Guest: Yes, it is Schubert, that's right, his "Unfinished Symphony No. 8." Okay, here's another, another team question for you, a team question, try this scramble anyone please. (*Gonzaga picks up their pencils.*) What is the largest city on the island of—

Gerry Beresford buzzes.

Bill Guest: Gerry?

Gerry Beresford: St. John's.

Bill Guest: That's not right. *(Tom Harrington wipes his hands as Gerry Beresford bows his head in despair.)* Alberta, what is the largest city on the island of Luzon?

Alberta consults. Pat Bendin buzzes as Bill Guest says:

Bill Guest: That's the time.

Pat Bendin: At one point, Ihor had a question, and instead of answering, he turned to us, to bring us together as a team, and the moderator said time.

Bill Guest: Manila is the answer. We'll go on to the next question.

Pat Bendin: And it went to Gonzaga.

Bill Guest: Try this one. Anyone. We have Canadians who have painted some very fine canvases, we want you to identify the artist in each case, who painted what you see on the monitor here, right now, please?

Image of A.Y. Jackson's The Red Maple *appears. Peter Chafe buzzes.*

Bill Guest: Peter?

Peter Chafe: A.Y. Jackson.

Bill Guest: That's who it is, *The Red Maple*.

Pat Bendin: That's when we lost the game.

Bill Guest: Now who painted this garden that you see? (*The painting by Arthur Lismer that appears cannot be identified from the old footage.*)

Tim Black buzzes.

Bill Guest: Tim?

Tim Black: I don't know.

Bill Guest: You don't know. Maybe Newfoundland knows. Anyone?

Peter Chafe buzzes.

Bill Guest: Peter?

Peter Chafe: Carmichael.

Bill Guest: No, the answer is Arthur Lismer. Now this work (*image of John Graham Coughtry's* Two Figure Series XIX, 1964 *appears*) was completed a decade ago, who was the artist?

Peter Chafe buzzes.

Bill Guest: Peter?

Peter Chafe: Soutine.

Bill Guest: That's not right. Do you know on the Alberta Team?

Tim Black buzzes.

Bill Guest: Tim?

Tim Black: Chirico.

Bill Guest: No it was Graham Coughtry that time, and finally, who painted this bird (*image of Norval Morrisseau's* Bird with Power *appears*) that you see here? Name of—

Peter Chafe buzzes.

Bill Guest: Peter?

Peter Chafe: Miro.

Bill Guest: No that's not right.

Tim Black buzzes.

Bill Guest: Tim?

Tim Black: Kenojuak.

Bill Guest: No, it was Norval Morrisseau. That was his *Bird with Power*.

Alberta 135
Newfoundland 225

Bill Guest: Okay teams, I'm going to give you the names of musical compositions, or the names of musicals, and you give me the composers if you can, please. First of all, who composed "Moon River" and—Brian.

Brian Mader: *(Opens his mouth, but nothing comes out.)*

Bill Guest: That won't do it. Newfoundland, "Moon River" and "Days of Wine and Roses."

Gerry Beresford: Foster?

Bill Guest: Gerry?

Gerry Beresford: Foster?

Bill Guest: No, the answer is Henry Mancini. Who composed "Anything Goes" and—yes, Gerry.

Gerry Beresford: Bernstein.

Bill Guest: That won't do it. "Anything Goes," Alberta, and "Can-Can." Yes, Brian.

Brian Mader: Offenbach?

Gerry Beresford: No, the answer is Cole Porter. Who wrote the musicals *Showboat* and *The Cat and the Fiddle*?

Tom Harrington buzzes.

Tom Harrington: Lerner and Loewe?

Bill Guest: That's not right. Do you know, Alberta, please? Brian?

Brian Mader: Ah, Rogers and Hammerstein.

Bill Guest: No, it was Jerome Kern who wrote *Showboat* and *The Cat and the Fiddle*. Who composed "My Old Kentucky Home" and—Brian.

Brian Mader: Foster.

Bill Guest: That's right, and "The Old Folks at Home." And who composed the song "Raindrops Keep Falling—"

Sethu Reddy buzzes.

Bill Guest: Yes, Sethu?

Sethu Reddy: Bert Bacharach.

Bill Guest: That's right, "...Falling on my Head," yes. Well, let's remain in the area of entertainment here, you could earn forty-five points if you get all of this question. Here is the scramble. In what movie did Groucho Marx play the part of Otis B. Driftwood? Anyone? Tim.

Tim Black: *Animal Crackers.*

Bill Guest: That's not right. Anyone with the Newfoundland team? The answer is, Gerry?

Gerry Beresford: Charlie Chaplain.

Bill Guest: No, it was *A Night at The Opera*. Okay, this is a multiple choice question on geography this time, good luck with these. Is a fosse, F-O-S-S-E, a ditch, a hill, a forest, or a rock?

Gerry Beresford buzzes.

Bill Guest: Which is it Gerry?

Gerry Beresford: A hill?

Bill Guest: It is not. Do you know, Alberta? Ihor.

Ihor Gowda: A rock.

Bill Guest: It is a ditch. (*Audience laughs.*) A friagem, a friagem, is a precious stone, a cold wave, a blue hole, or a flower? What is it, Peter?

Peter Chafe: A blue hole.

Bill Guest: It is not. Do you know, Tim?

Tim Black: A cold wind.

Bill Guest: It is a cold wave[1]—yes, I guess you misunderstood, but you're quite right, yes. Is a freshet—he probably misunderstood me, judges, but I think he's pretty close there—is a freshet a clear stream, a fish, a thin frog, or a wreath? Go ahead, Brian.

Alberta 155
Newfoundland 235

Brian Mader: A wreath.

Bill Guest: It is not. Do you know, Sethu?

Sethu Reddy: A clear stream.

Bill Guest: It is a clear stream, yes. A haboob, haboob, is a swift current, a sluggish lake, a narrow channel, or a dust storm. What is it, Brian?

Brian Mader: A dust storm.

Bill Guest: It is a dust storm. That's what it is, yes. Let's visit the public library here. These books that I'm about

---

[1] A friagem is not a wave in a nautical sense, but a meteorological one: it is a cold spell accompanied by cold winds.

to mention are prominent in the fields of psychology and psychiatry. I'll give you the title; you give me the author if you can. Here's the first one, it's open. Who wrote *The Theory of Psychoanalysis*. Who was that, Peter?

Peter Chafe: Freud.

Bill Guest: That was not right. Yes Tim Black?

Tim Black: Jung.

Bill Guest: It was Carl Gustav Jung, yes. Who wrote *The Practice and Theory of Individual Psychology*? Brian?

Brian Mader: Freud.

Bill Guest: No. Do you know, Newfoundland? Anyone? Peter?

Alberta 175
Newfoundland 245

Peter Chafe: Bacon.

Bill Guest: It was Alfred Adler. A recent bestseller, who wrote *I'm O*—yes, Tim?

Tim Black: Harris.

Bill Guest: That's right, *I'm OK—You're OK*, Thomas Harris. Who wrote *Man's Search for Meaning*? Who did that? Yes, Tim.

Tim Black: Fromme.

Bill Guest: That is not right. Do you know, Gerry?

Gerry Beresford: Freud?

Alberta 185
Newfoundland 245

Bill Guest: Viktor E. Frankl. And finally, who was the author of *The Interpretation of Dreams*? Who was that, Sethu?

Sethu Reddy: Freud.

Bill Guest: It was. Sigmund Freud is quite right, yes.

Alberta 185
Newfoundland 255

Bill Guest: Now, what do you know about modern history? Try these. In 1945—Gerry?

Gerry Beresford: The end of ... (*he stammers into incoherence.*)

Bill Guest: Come on, you can do it.

Gerry Beresford: (*Slams his fist on the desk.*)

Bill Guest: I'll give this to Alberta. One of the best answers I've heard so far though, Gerry. Alberta, try this. (*Tom Harrington and Sethu Reddy try and calm Gerry Beresford down.*)

In 1945, the big three powers met on the Crimean Peninsula to discuss plans for post-war Europe. The conference was named after what city?

Brian Mader buzzes.

Bill Guest: Brian?

Brian Mader: Yalta.

Bill Guest: Right on, for ten points, yes. Open question, both teams again. Franklin Delano Roosevelt and Winston Churchill represented the United States and Britain—go ahead, Tom.

Tom Harrington: Stalin.

Bill Guest: Yes, he represented The USSR to round out the three. One of the most controversial Yalta deals ceded three bordering Baltic countries—yes, Brian?

Brian Mader: Lithuania, Estonia, and Latvia.

Alberta 205
Newfoundland 265

Bill Guest: Now that is right on. Yes indeed, they were bordering on the USSR. Now the first big-three conference had been held in 1943 in what city? Yes, Gerry.

Gerry Beresford: Potsdam.

Bill Guest: That is not right. Do you know, Pat? (*Pat Bendin takes too long to answer.*) The answer is Tehran. Now here's a multiple-choice question again, and what have we this time? (*a glitch in the recording*) language, and I think you'll enjoy this one. (*A bell rings.*) As a matter of fact we won't get to it, (*all players react*)[2] these are the short snappers, and they are open. Here is the first of them. Who was known as the poet of the Yukon? Who was that, Ihor?

Ihor Gowda: Service.

Bill Guest: That's right. In which city will you find McGill University? Which one, Pat?

Pat Bendin: Montreal.

Alberta 215
Newfoundland 265

Bill Guest: That's correct, for ten points. What date do we celebrate Canada Day? Go ahead, Pat.

Pat Bendin: July 1st.

Bill Guest: That's right. How many years old is Canada this year? Pat?

---

2 Incidentally, none of the players remember being able to see the scores; they weren't aware of how close it was nor how little time was left.

Pat Bendin: 107.

Bill Guest: That's right. What kind of a bird is a brant? What kind, Pat?

Pat Bendin: A swan.

Bill Guest: That is not right, do you know, Peter?

Peter Chafe: A seagull.

Bill Guest: It is a goose. Try this for ten points. Simple Simon went a-fishing—yes, ah, Gerry?

Gerry Beresford: Pie man?

Bill Guest: No. Simple Simon went a-fishing to catch a what, Tim? Tim, it's yours.

Alberta 245
Newfoundland 260

Tim Black: Fish.

Bill Guest: No, it was a whale, as a matter of fact. What line is at approximately twenty-three and a half degrees—yes, Pat.

Pat Bendin: Capricorn.

Alberta 255
Newfoundland 260

Bill Guest: Yes, of latitude. A sandbar extending outward from the shore is called what? Go ahead, Pat.

Pat Bendin: A delta.

Bill Guest: It is not, no. Do you know, Peter?

Peter Chafe: A barachois.

Bill Guest: It is called—yes, a barachois, you're quite right.

Loud applause, excitement from the audience. Tom Harrington and Sethu Reddy, aware they are running out of time, wave their hands to calm the crowd.

Alberta 255
Newfoundland 270

Bill Guest: Who explored the coast of Newfoundland for Portugal—yes, Brian.

Brian Mader: (*Tries to say Cabot.*)

Bill Guest: In 15—Who was that, Gerry?

Tom Harrington, Sethu Reddy, and Gerry Beresford all answer Corte Real.

Bill Guest: Just one answer at a time, please. I'm going to rule it out, out says the judge. (*Reaction from Tom Harrington and Gerry Beresford.*) In area, which is the largest US state?

Which is it, Peter?

Peter Chafe: (*Seems to back away from his answer.*) Washington.

Bill Guest: That won't do. Do you know, Alberta?

Ihor Gowda: Alaska.

Bill Guest: It is Alaska, yes.

Alberta 265
Newfoundland 270

Bill Guest: Until February 1974, who led the movement on Cyprus for reunion with Greece? Who was that, please, Ihor?

Ihor Gowda: Archbishop Makarios.

Bill Guest: That will not do. Do you know, Newfoundland? It was Grivas. Franklin Roosevelt's presidency began in what year? What year, Pat?

Pat Bendin: 1933.

Alberta 270
Newfoundland 270

Bill Guest: That's right on, yes. Who was United States Commander-in-Chief in the Pacific—yes, Pat?

Pat Bendin: (*Clicks fingers, but can't get anything out.*)

Alberta 270
Newfoundland 270

Bill Guest: Try it, please, in World War II, Newfoundland. Peter?

Peter Chafe: MacArthur.

Bill Guest: It was MacArthur, yes.

Applause, which is very loud; Gerry Beresford waves his hands and commands the crowd to "shut up."

Gerry Beresford: I remember telling people to be quiet, in a rude manner. My objective there was, Look, we got to be fair here. If we get an answer, you can't cheer and prevent somebody else from answering the next question. [It was about] trying to be sure the playing field was level.

Alberta 270
Newfoundland 280

Bill Guest: The faculties of Literature and Science at the University of Paris are called what? Go ahead, Ihor.

Ihor Gowda: Sorbonne.

Bill Guest: Sorbonne is right.

Alberta 275
Newfoundland 280

Bill Guest: For ten points, what is a cheroot? A cheroot, Ihor.

Ihor Gowda: It's a bird.

Bill Guest: It is not. Gerry?

Gerry Beresford: A fish?

Bill Guest: It is a cigar. Who wrote the tale about Flopsy, Mopsy, Cottontail, and—yes, Peter?

Peter Chafe: Potter.

Bill Guest: No, it was—yes, it was Potter, Beatrix Potter. Who was the good wizard in Tolkien's *Lord*—yes, Brian?

Brian Mader: Merlin. (*Puts hand on head, knows it is wrong.*)

Bill Guest: No, in *Lord of the Rings*, who was it, please, Newfoundland. You know, Peter?

Peter Chafe: [unclear]

Bill Guest: It was Gandalf.

Gerry Beresford: And I remember the last answer.

Bill Guest: What is the most common word in written English. The most common—Peter?

Gerry Beresford: The last answer was the word *the*.

Peter Chafe: The.

Gerry Beresford: And the way Peter said it.

Bill Guest: That—that's right, *the*.

Gerry Beresford: Peter said the word *the*.

Bill Guest: For ten points–

Siren goes, and the audience erupts.

Gerry Beresford: And then the buzzer went, and I leapt up.

Alberta 275
Newfoundland 300

Tom Harrington and Sethu Reddy embrace. Gerry Beresford throws himself in with them.

Gerry Beresford: And I remember just being totally ecstatic.

The crowd is making too much noise to hear Bill Guest. But he is heard saying, "Newfoundland are the new, 1974, champions."

Alberta 275
Newfoundland 300

Bill Guest: It's official. The new *Reach for the Top* champions, the team representing Newfoundland. And it's all over for the second best team in Canada, Alberta, but when you reach this point, you're champions in your own right.

Bill Guest reintroduces the Gonzaga team.

Bill Guest: The crown is yours, fellows, wear it proudly. You're the best *Reach for the Top* team in Canada.

Gerry Beresford: *(off camera)* They're all good.

Bill Guest: They're all good. Okay, Gerry, you said it.

Gerry Beresford: Peter Chafe was the finest *Reach for the Top* player: he was cool. At the end there were three people hugging, and he was still sitting there, cool.

Bill Guest: And goodbye from St. John's.

The Reach for the Top *logo is projected as the theme music plays and the credits roll.*

CBC logo with symbols of a Newfoundland dog and film reels.

SCENE SIX

LIFTED UP, LOOKING AHEAD

Tim Black: Our final score was quite a bit less than what we'd been getting. I do remember Ihor getting the same number of points as the rest of us, and we were used to him getting much more.

John Perlin: *Front Page Challenge* also taped some shows in St. John's.

Tim Black: It would have helped us if we'd had some tougher games before, had to fight back from a deficit.

Pat Bendin: The last night, after we had lost the game, we had never lost before…But I don't remember being down for very long.

Ihor Gowda: All of us guys, we had a great time in Newfoundland.

Pat Bendin: We didn't sleep.

Tom Harrington: It was a Friday night, and I was up all night, and we were on the front page of *The Evening Telegram*. Well, my father [Michael Harrington] was Editor-in-Chief. My parents took me to the Starboard Quarter.[1]

Tim Black: We had lunch with the mayor,[2] who was a real character.

Pat Bendin: I remember a meeting with Dorothy Wyatt. She was quite a lively lady. I can't be sure about this, but I remember she wore different coloured hosiery on each leg.

Tim Black: She was a woman of a certain age, and she was wearing fishnet stockings. At the time, we had the most boring mayor on earth [Ivor Dent].

Tom Harrington: Everyone stayed in MUN residence, including us.

Gerry Beresford: Tom's roommate was from PEI, Michael, which turned out to be Michaela, so he ended up with a room to himself.

Tom Harrington: I had a crush on a girl from Northern Ontario.

---

[1] As referenced earlier by Bill Rowe, considered the finest of St. John's (then few) restaurants.
[2] Dorothy Wyatt, née Fanning, 1925-2001

Gerry Beresford: We made really good friends.

Sethu Reddy: We stayed in residence in Memorial for that week.[3] I didn't even tell my parents we'd won; they were shocked [when they saw the game].

Gerry Beresford: On Sunday the 14th of July, Father Ed Bromley hosted a show on VOWR, and we were his guests. My father called me after the show, to say how he was proud of us.

Edward Roberts: I spent 1974 campaigning for leader, and won.

Bill Rowe: I spent the year in the South of France with my family. We were in Grasse, the perfume capital of the world.

Gerry Beresford: And the next day my father went to Boston for his operation. That's the last thing I remember talking to my dad about.

As the winning team, Gonzaga was offered a choice between a trip to London or Paris, or a trip to Stony Mountain, Alberta, with two other ranking teams; they had chosen Alberta, and Bob Cole had presented them with sleeping bags, on air.

Gerry Beresford: Everyone thought we were crazy.

---

3 The shows were taped, so the Gonzaga team knew they were the champions, but kept their secret until after the game was broadcast.

Tom Harrington: We went to Alberta. We opted to go to Alberta. We slept in teepees, we rode horses, we prepared a deer hide. I've been to Paris and London many times since, but I've never done anything like that.

Gerry Beresford: It was the right move.

Tom Harrington: The girl from Northern Ontario was there. On the way back [from Alberta] we stopped in Toronto.

Gerry Beresford: The Jesuits hosted us for a week.

Tom Harrington: We were on the lunchtime talk show *Elwood Glover*.

Gerry Beresford: We appeared on *The Elwood Glover Show*, and he asked us to name the seven dwarfs. I think we got three.

Tom Harrington: And the other guest was Jon Voight.

Gerry Beresford: Jon Voight was on that show. It was kind of neat.

Tom Harrington: We were in the green room with him, and he was really interested, asking questions.

Bill Rowe: It was all part of the wild and wooly attitude.

Edward Roberts: And then I began to hear noises, that there was "public demand" that Mr. Smallwood had to come back, that he was organizing his own political party, and this became the Liberal Reform Party.

Bill Rowe: The reason I went over there [the south of France] was to learn some French, to do some courses, but also because I felt myself part of what was happening, the renaissance that was happening.

Edward Roberts: All it really did was re-elect Moores.[4] Would we have won if it had been Moores and myself? I believe we would have, but make your own guess.

Bill Rowe: You'd fly EPA to Gander, and then you had to hang around the airport in Gander for hours. You would dress to travel, you wouldn't think about wearing your jeans on the plane; I wouldn't be surprised if I had a shirt and tie and a suit on, and Penny would have been dressed to the nines.

John Perlin: I took a helicopter to Bay d'Espoir. What we would do was go in and meet the community group who was going to do the dinner. In Bay d'Espoir, it was a women's parish group. We asked what they wanted to serve, and they said pan-fried cod. That was fine. We asked what wine they would serve, and they said Baby Duck, or Cold Duck.

Bill Rowe: Every friend you had around Christmas time had a big, massive cocktail party. So you spent the whole two weeks going from house to house, getting half-drunk with people

---

4 The election of September 16, 1975, elected 30 Conservatives, 16 Liberals, and 5 Reform Liberals.

you'd seen the night before, the week before. There was a lot of camaraderie.

John Perlin: We said, well, you'll need to be a little more upscale than that.

Bill Rowe: Nobody minded whether you had a few drinks and drove a car in those days. Shocking kinds of attitudes to this day and age. New Year's Eve at Bally Haly was a big deal. Coming out at three or four o'clock in the morning, everybody half-polluted, in a big snowstorm, people skidding through drifts.

John Perlin: Liebfraumilch was the height of sophistication in those days, so we suggested that.

Bill Rowe: I went over to write the first draft of my first novel.

Edward Roberts: I don't know what motivated him [Smallwood].

John Perlin: The culmination was the twenty-fifth anniversary dinner held in Gander during Prince Philip's visit to the Gander/Botwood area.

Bill Rowe: I spent the whole nine months on *Clapp's Rock*: 1500 typed pages! Editors got a hold of it, and with their guidance I produced a nice little novel.

Edward Roberts: I believe it was two things. He couldn't stomach the idea of anybody else leading. And secondly, I and my colleagues were not as enamoured as he was, we were unenamoured, with the deals with Shaheen and Doyle.[5] We didn't leave the cabinet; we believed we could do more inside the cabinet than out, and we did. Come-by-Chance and the Stephenville linerboard mill were disasters.

John Crosbie: At a distance, I realize that there are lots of reasons [Smallwood] had turned out as he turned out. I am no longer so angry and disgusted, but I have no warm feelings for him except he was a patriotic Newfoundlander.

Bill Rowe: I consider myself part of the psychology of what was happening in Newfoundland at that time, that same mentality. These guys [the Gonzaga *Reach for the Top* team] were savvy, and competent, and confident.

Gerry Beresford: The Jesuit influence on my life has continued, and it started there. They were very, very supportive then to me.

Pat Bendin: What's left is mostly impressions. My experience of St. John's was that it was old, [built of] wood, friendly. Colder than I thought it would be. People spoke differently.

Gerry Beresford: 1974 was a big year in terms of my personal life; two weeks after we had won *Reach for the Top,* my dad died.

---

5 John M. Shaheen, an American businessman and one of the principal funders of Richard Nixon's 1968 presidential campaign, orchestrated the Come-by-Chance oil refinery. The project's 1976 bankruptcy was then the biggest in Canadian history. John C. Doyle, a Chicago-born entrepreneur, was involved in several Smallwood-era natural resource projects of which the linerboard mill was particularly ruinous, costing Newfoundland an estimated $122 million and ranking as the biggest white-collar crime in provincial history.

Tom Harrington: At sixteen you're still figuring out who you are.

Gerry Beresford: It was sudden. He had gone to Boston for a gallbladder operation and gotten an infection from the operation and passed away.

Sethu Reddy: The game is all a blur. I recently saw part of it on YouTube. We built up a tremendous lead in the first half. In the end, Peter thankfully answered two or three questions.

Pat Bendin: I found [the championship game] on YouTube, to my surprise. My first impression is it was not as I remembered it. My memory is not so much about the game. Most of my memory is being in St. John's.

Gerry Beresford: And the Jesuit priests who were there [at Gonzaga] lifted me up and carried me through that difficult time.

Pat Bendin: What is left with me is I wish I had expressed more gratitude as a student for the effort of the teachers. I was lucky enough to be at the National Debate Competition that year as well, and it was the same thing. The teachers did so much, and I didn't appreciate it as a student as much as I should have.

Tom Harrington: The provincial government had a luncheon for us.

Gerry Beresford: In September 1974, the premier, Frank

Moores, invited us and our families to dine with him and some members of his cabinet.

Tom Harrington: The premier spoke.

Gerry Beresford: He gave us a medal.

John Perlin: The provincial government struck these medallions, with the provincial coat of arms on one side and the twenty-fifth anniversary of Confederation on the other.

Pat Bendin: The impression that Newfoundlanders had become Canadians a different way than we had.

John Perlin: I was in boarding school in Ontario in 1949, and the Canadians had no idea. They thought they were doing us a big favour. Up until the oil arrived. And now oil has declined. I wonder, will we see the same kind of patronizing attitudes?

John Crosbie: We're going to have tough times again. It's going to be very difficult.

John Perlin: The people did benefit. But it was a loss of sovereignty. Businesses were closing and there were—the carpetbaggers, I call them, like in the American south after the Civil War, except there was no war here, except for a war of words.

John Crosbie: If I had listened to my father [Chesley Crosbie] and taken his advice and not run for [Smallwood], things could have been quite different.

Sethu Reddy: We all went on to do something different: Peter, engineering; Tom, journalism; myself, medicine; and Gerry, commerce and business. We were a good mix.

Tom Harrington: When I first was with CBC, I was sports. I knew I had weaknesses, but I knew one of my strengths was I could absorb information quickly and retain it. In sports that's particularly important. I got that from *Reach for the Top*.

Sethu Reddy: At Gonzaga, we had so many bright students, but they didn't advertise. That was the culture, a good trait to have.

Tim Black: Sethu and I corresponded for a long time. He was lovely. He signed his letters, "Your friend, Sethu."

John Crosbie: I made mistakes. There's no one who doesn't make mistakes. But it was all very interesting.

Ken Coffey: I actually watched [the 1974] games at the old Hoyles Home, visiting my wife's great aunt. It was such a feeling of pride.

Brian Mader: I work with a lot of Newfoundlanders. It's nice to have this starting point.

Sethu Reddy: *Reach for the Top* was a very popular show. In those days, we had only two channels. But I'm still puzzled, even mystified, when I go back to Newfoundland—people still remember.

Edward Roberts: That was 1974.

Gonzaga remains the only team from Newfoundland to win the *Reach for the Top* national championship.

CAST NOTES

PATRICK BENDIN earned degrees from the University of Alberta and the London School of Economics. He has lived in Ottawa and worked with the federal department of justice for more than fifteen years. He is married with three children.

GERRY BERESFORD did a commerce degree at MUN, and was accepted to study law at Osgoode Hall when he took a year to work on a fisheries industry survey. He later completed an MBA at Queens and worked for FPI until 2001, then shifting to the energy industry. He was Project Administration Manager, Newfoundland Transshipment Limited before being appointed Chief Administrative Officer at Commission of Inquiry Respecting the Muskrat Falls Project. Beresford is married with two daughters.

When **TIM BLACK** went to university he intended to study optical physics, but veered into English literature and philosophy. After working as a technical writer, he spent twenty-five years in software design with Honeywell. He lives in Edmonton with his partner and their children.

PETER CHAFE lives in Toronto.

KEN COFFEY was a student at Gonzaga from 1967 to 1970. He returned in 1975 as a chemistry teacher, and later acting vice-principal. His extracurricular work included drama and *Reach for the Top*. In Coffey's days as a student, enrollment was so high the students attended in three shifts: (A) 8:30-2:30; (B) 8:30-11:10 and 3:10 to 6; and (C) 11:30-6. This proved so unpopular, partly because it caused so much trouble for organized sports, that students went on strike in September 1968 and marched to the Confederation building. The authorities agreed to discontinue the experiment and the next year returned to the 9-3 schedule.

JOHN CROSBIE is a former provincial and federal politician, cabinet member, and candidate for federal PC party leader; the former twelfth lieutenant-governor of Newfoundland and Labrador; and author of *No Holds Barred: My Life in Politics*. Between 1972 and 1976, he was Minister of Finances, Minister of Fisheries, Minister of Mines and Energy, and Government House Leader under Premier Frank Moores.

After high school, **IHOR GOWDA** studied computer science at the University of Alberta and UBC. He worked in telecommunications until he decided to try something new, semi-retired, and moved to Austin, TX. He worked in the music business and has written a play, *Poison*, about a fictional meeting between Alan Turing and Robert Oppenheimer, which debuted in the fall 2015. He is single with no children.

TOM HARRINGTON has hosted and guest hosted many of CBC's flagship radio and television programs, including *Marketplace*, *As It Happens*, and *The World This Hour*. He lives in Toronto and is married with one daughter.

JOHN PERLIN was the Director of Cultural Affairs and in 1974 oversaw the twenty-fifth anniversary celebrations on behalf of the province. Since retirement he has been awarded the Order of Newfoundland and Labrador for his extensive work with charities, including the Vera Perlin Society and the Royal St. John's Regatta.

BRIAN MADER studied languages, including French and Russian, and is now employed with the government of Alberta working with people with complex disabilities.

EDWARD ROBERTS is a former provincial politician and Liberal Party leader and was the eleventh lieutenant-governor of Newfoundland and Labrador. He has published several books, including *A Blue Puttee at War: The Memoirs of Captain Sydney Frost*, from Flanker Press.

BILL ROWE is a former politician, public commentator, lawyer, and broadcaster. In 2011 he retired from VOCM to concentrate on his writing. The author of several books of fiction and non-fiction, his most recent publications include *The Premiers Joey and Frank* and *The Worst and the Best of the Premiers and Some We Never Had*, both from Flanker Press.

REFERENCES

Crosbie, John C. *No Holds Barred: My Life in Politics*. Toronto: McClelland & Stewart, 1997.

The transcriptions for the 1974 *Reach for the Top* national championship were created using video of the program available on YouTube: http://www.youtube.com/watch?v=JMergow-ELg and https://www.youtube.com/watch?v=NhWgdTv3g0E.

Joan Sullivan lives and works in St. John's, where she is editor of *Newfoundland Quarterly* and contributes cultural articles and obituaries to local and national publications. Her writing includes *In the Field*, *The Long Run*, and, as a playwright, the theatre script *Rig: The Ocean Ranger* and the stage adaptation of Wayne Johnston's *The Story of Bobby O'Malley*. *In the Field* won the 2013 Rogers Communication Award for Non-fiction.